DELAWARE

A Turner Educational Services, Inc. book. Based on the Portrait
of America television series created by R.E. (Ted) Turner.

Library of Congress Number: 86-17677

345678910   99989796959493929190

Library of Congress Cataloging in Publication Data

Thompson, Kathleen.
  Delaware.

  (Portrait of America)
  "A Turner book."
  Summary: Discusses the history, economy, culture,
and future of Delaware. Includes a chronology, section
on state statistics, and maps showing counties and
physical features.
  1. Delaware—Juvenile literature. [1. Delaware]
I. Title. II. Series: Thompson, Kathleen.
Portrait of America.
F164.3.T48   1986   975.1   86-17677
ISBN 0-86514-450-8 (lib. bdg.)
ISBN 0-86514-525-3 (softcover)

Cover Photo: Delaware Department of Natural Resources

★ ★ ★ ★ ★
Portrait of AMERICA

DELAWARE

Kathleen Thompson

A TURNER BOOK
RAINTREE PUBLISHERS

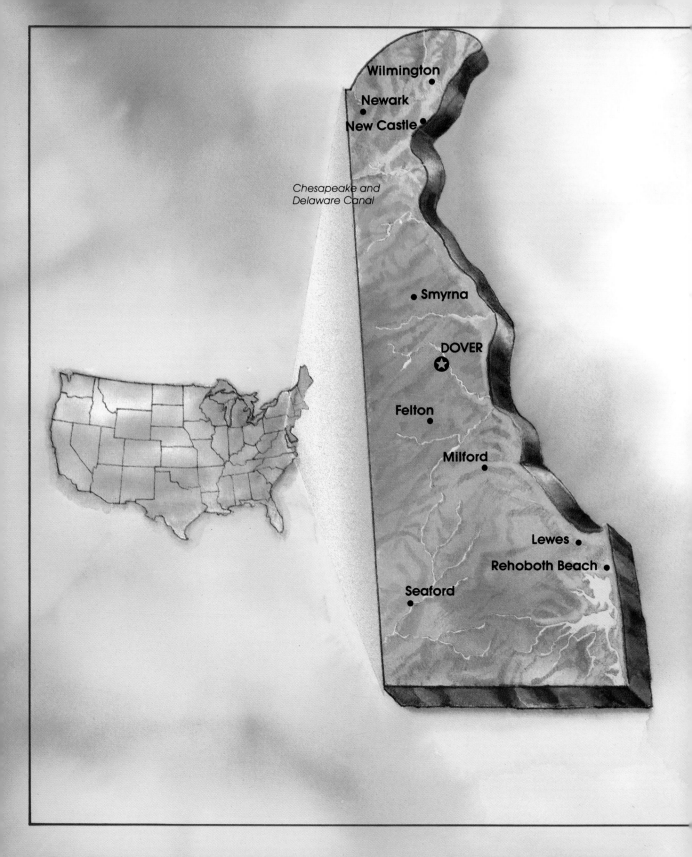

Wilmington

Newark

New Castle

Chesapeake and
Delaware Canal

Smyrna

DOVER

Felton

Milford

Lewes

Rehoboth Beach

Seaford

CONTENTS

Introduction

Delaware, the First State.

". . . haven't we really lost the personal touch? . . . But here in Delaware (people) can get it, because they have shaken hands with their governor, with their congressman, with their senator."

Delaware: chemicals, beaches, a chicken in every pot.

". . . Delawareans really have an attitude that they like to grow where they're planted."

Delaware is a small state. But, as people have begun to discover in the modern world, small is beautiful. Small is powerful, creative, ingenious. Unique solutions to problems that wouldn't work in a bigger state work in Delaware. Barriers between people find it difficult to grow.

Delaware is small, but it works.

Lewes, the traditional home of pilots who guide ships up Delaware Bay.

The First State

On a stormy day in 1610, Samuel Argall took shelter from the fierce Atlantic in a bay about midway down the east coast of the North American continent. He was an English explorer from the colony of Virginia. And he was lost. In the great tradition of explorers who think they have found something new, Argall gave the bay a name. He called it the De La Warr Bay, after the governor of Virginia, Lord De La Warr.

The truth of the matter is, Argall was not the first person to discover the area we now call Delaware. For one thing, Henry Hudson had been there the year before. But more importantly, the land belonged to an old and respected people, the Leni-Lenape Indians.

This is a modern sailing ship in Delaware Bay, named De La Warr Bay in 1610 by Samuel Argall.

An early explorer described the Leni-Lenape, later called the Delaware Indians, this way. They were "proper and shapely, very swift, their language lofty. They speak little, but fervently and with great elegancy. I have never seen more natural sagacity." But the sagacity, or wisdom, of the Leni-Lenape did not save them from the diseases and the guns of the European settlers.

In 1631, the Dutch founded a settlement near the present town of Lewes. They named it Zwaanendael. But Dutch attitudes toward the land and its resources were very different from those of the Indians. And the Leni-Lenape resisted this first attempt to take their homeland from them. The settlement lasted only one year.

Seven years later, a permanent settlement was established near the present town of Wilmington. The New Sweden Company, under the leadership of Peter Minuit, built Fort Christina. The New Sweden colony had both Dutch and Swedish

This is an etching of a Leni-Lanape family.

colonists. Those from Sweden were apparently better able to deal with the hardships of the Delaware weather, and soon the colony was primarily Swedish.

The Dutch government, however, believed that the colony was in Dutch territory. They built Fort Casimir just north of New Sweden and attempted to take over the settlement. Then the Swedes captured Fort Casimir. And then the Dutch took it back. By 1665, New Sweden was part of New Netherland, the Dutch outpost in the new world.

The struggle for Delaware did not end there, however. Soon the English got into the act. The English wanted to control all trade in America and the Dutch were making inroads. The English sent a fleet of ships to capture the Dutch forts. In 1664, Delaware became a part of the English province of New York.

It was eighteen years before another major change occurred in the government of Delaware. William Penn was looking for a connection between his colony of Pennyslvania and the Atlantic Ocean. In 1681, the Duke of York gave him Delaware. But Penn respected the identity of this small region and did not simply swallow it up. In fact, in 1704, he allowed Delaware to create its own legislature. Although Pennsylvania governors continued to oversee the affairs of Delaware, the people of these three counties made their own laws.

As the unrest that would lead to the American Revolution began in the colonies, Delaware was torn. Many people were still loyal to England. Of Delaware's three delegates to the Continental Congress, one voted for independence and one against and the third, Caesar Rodney, rode from Dover to Philadelphia "through a severe summer storm" to break the tie. Once the vote was cast, however, all three delegates signed the Declaration of Independence.

And then the war began. In 1777, Delaware was invaded by British forces who were on their way from the Chesapeake Bay to Philadelphia. Washington's army was ready for them at Wilmington, but the British swerved around them and entered Pennsylvania. Washington followed them and was de-feated at the Battle of Brandywine in September of 1777.

The British captured Wilmington and, eventually, all the forts along the Delaware River. With the British in control of the river, the capital was moved inland, from New Castle to Dover.

After the war came the organization of a new country. Delaware was very active. The size of this small state made its people realize that they needed a strong

union for protection. In fact, Delaware was so eager that it was the first state to ratify the Constitution of the United States.

The new country offered great opportunities. And the Delaware River provided water power for all kinds of mills. An industrial empire was founded in 1802 when E.I. du Pont built a gunpowder mill on the banks of the Brandywine Creek near Wilmington. It would one day become one of the biggest chemical companies in the world. And the Du Ponts would be a power in Delaware throughout its history.

Delaware itself was a powerful part of the economic center of the new United States. In a few years, much of that power would shift towards New York. But Delaware would remain an important state because of its location and the business talent of its people.

The Du Pont powder mill on Brandywine Creek.

Delaware's loyalty to the Union was tested with the War of 1812. Its congressmen were against the war and tried to prevent it. But once war was declared, Delaware supported the federal government.

It was during this war that a British commander discovered how hard it was to attack the fishing village of Lewes. The British fleet aimed 241 cannons at the town for almost a month. Incendiary rockets were launched from the British ships. They missed. Almost all of them. One lone rocket managed to hit its target, but it didn't explode. Finally, the British left in a huff, having killed one chicken.

The attack on Lewes was the only direct attack on Delaware during the entire war.

During the 1800s, industry grew in Delaware and with it the transportation system. Turnpikes and toll roads were laid out, and canals were built. The shipyard and mills brought in more people, eager to work. Slavery, which had once been useful to Delaware's agricultural economy, began to fade out—but not entirely.

When the Civil War broke out, Delaware was still a slave state. But it had much more in common with its northern neighbors—historically and economically—than with the southern states. There was never any real possibility that Delaware would withdraw from the union, and it

didn't. However, soldiers from the state fought in both armies. Delaware's position during the Civil War was never completely clear. And a look at a map shows that Delaware is the only state that lies, not south or north of the Mason-Dixon line, but east of it.

After the war, the federal government punished Delaware for its divided loyalties—and pushed the state solidly into the southern camp for years. Because of its southern loyalties, Delaware was a Democratic stronghold until the turn of the century. After that, black people began to use the vote that had previously been denied them. From 1900 to 1936, Delaware became strongly Republican. When Democrat Franklin D. Roosevelt came along and won the hearts of the American people by getting them through the hard times of the Great Depression, Delaware finally became a real two-party state.

All this time, industry—especially Du Pont—was thriving. Wilmington was a center of industrial growth and wealth. The population of the state boomed as more and more immigrants came looking for work. In 1951, the Delaware Memorial Bridge was built to connect the state with New Jersey. Still more factories—and more people—flooded across the bridge.

Two decades later, Delaware was facing a slowing economy. But new tax laws and other incentives changed that trend. Today 52 percent of the Fortune 500 companies—the country's largest and wealthiest—have offices in Delaware.

That's the interesting thing about Delaware. In the history of the United States, and in today's business world, Delaware plays a role that sometimes seems out of proportion to its size. It's small, but it's mighty.

At the left is the Delaware Memorial Bridge. The inset shows the bridge during construction.

Nettie Horn working at a spinning wheel.

Is Progress a Parking Lot?

"I can still close my eyes now and say this is the house here and that was the house there. These people lived here, and they had two children. I went to school with one of them. The Sherman Marvels were next door. The Pooles were at the corner. Across the street were the Moores. Later was Mrs. Englehardt. Later on there was somebody else. . . . And now I live in the middle of a parking lot. Cars next door, cars in front of me, cars on the west of me. And I sup-

pose I'll be walled in if I live for another five years."

Nettie Horn has lived in Rehoboth, Delaware, for ninety years. Things have changed a lot in that time.

The word *Rehoboth* means "room enough." Nettie Horn wonders how long there will be room enough for people to live gracefully, peacefully, with an appreciation of their community and each other. If that's the way people still want to live.

"The automobile has changed everyone's lives. The way they live, the way they think, the way they spend. Because if gasoline was five dollars a gallon, they'd go just the same. Because they're in the habit of spending the weekend somewhere. Doesn't make a difference whether it's close at home or far away. They've just got to get away from home for the weekend."

Home for Nettie Horn has never been a place you want to get away from. That feeling is one you find a lot among the older people of southern Delaware and many of the younger ones as well.

To those people, southern Delaware means the shore and the marsh. It means a way of life that has led the people of lower Delaware to call it "Slower Delaware." It means, to Nettie Horn, not giving away too much in the name of progress.

"Mary Meckle's house was a beautiful summer house, lovely porches all around, just a lovely, lovely house. The bulldozers came in and knocked it down. In the afternoon, they loaded it on trucks and practically just threw it away.

"Well, I don't know what progress is, really. Does anybody know really what progress is? Because it takes so much away from people when you have . . . these new things coming in."

Nettie Horn's home is the one in front of the yellow car.

The Tiny Giant

The little state along the Delaware River is, in its own way, an industrial giant. The two major reasons for this can be stated simply. They are Du Pont and corporation laws.

Delaware has gone out of its way to attract business and industry. In the past decade or so, state taxes have been cut, and the Delaware legislature has made it easy for companies to incorporate in their state. The result is that more than 250 corporations have offices here. In fact, more than half of the Fortune 500 corporations have offices in this small Eastern state.

And when you talk about Delaware's economy, you have to talk about Du Pont. It's a big company in a small state—and it shows. In fact, Du Pont is the twelfth largest corpora-

The Delaware River in winter.

Courtesy of C.P.C. General Motors Wilmington, Delaware

tion in the United States while Delaware is the 49th largest state. From its beginning as a gunpowder mill on the Delaware River to its present status as the world's largest chemical corporation, the Du Pont Company has played a big part in the economic development of Delaware. In 1973, Ralph Nader calculated that Du Pont generated

Photos by Du Pont

21 percent of the gross state product.

Chemicals are the leading area of manufacturing in Delaware. And Delaware, like most other Eastern states, is primarily a manufacturing state. About 85 percent of the value of goods

Delaware's industry is represented here by an auto assembly plant (above, left), a research scientist (below, left), and a technician who is checking fiber structure by computerized image analysis.

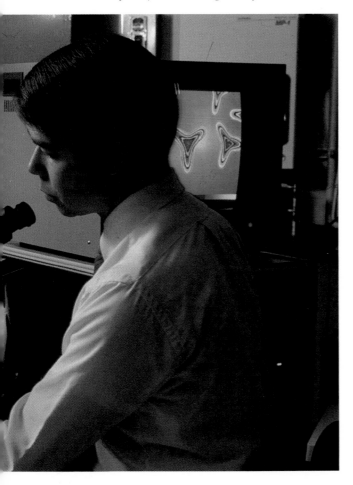

produced in Delaware comes from manufacturing. About one-fourth of that is accounted for by chemicals.

But Delaware is actually more important in chemical research than in chemical manufacturing. Many of Du Pont's manufacturing plants are located in other parts of the country and the world. But their research center near Wilmington is one of the largest in the world. And Du Pont is not the only chemical company in the state.

Next to chemicals, the largest area of manufacturing is food products. About one-sixth of the value of manufactured goods comes from the fruit-packing and canning plants around the state.

Delaware factories also produce paper products and a variety of other goods. There are large automobile assembly plants in Newark and Wilmington.

One advantage to all of these industries is Delaware's location. Because of the number of cities in the area, Delaware is within 500 miles of 70 million people, one-third of the nation's population.

About half of Delaware is farm-land. And the key word in agri-culture is chickens. Broiling chickens are the leading cash crop. Delaware ranks eighth na-tionally in broiler production, but no county in the United States raises more chickens than Sussex.

The modern poultry industry was born in Delaware sixty years ago when a woman named Cecile Steele had a simple, but very important, idea. Until that time, chickens for eating had been a by-product of the fresh egg industry. Steele decided to raise chickens the year round for the express purpose of selling them for eating.

Besides chickens, Delaware grows chicken feed. About 90 percent of Delaware's tilled farmland is used for soybeans and corn, which are used to feed the chickens.

A small percentage of Dela-ware's income comes from min-ing and fishing.

And many of Delaware's citi-zens are employed in occupa-tions that do not yield a product that you can see and touch. Because of all those corporate offices, more and more of the people in Delaware work in management positions in com-panies like 3M Business Pro-ducts, American Life Insurance Company, and Sears, Roebuck and Company. As a result, the average income in Delaware is about six percent higher than the national average. In fact, Delaware ranks ninth in the nation in per capita personal income.

Office of Ag Communications Delaware Cooperative Extension Service

Shown below is a broiler house. The worker above is checking the temperature in a broiler house. Fruit packing (right) and wheat (below) are also parts of Delaware's agricultural production.

Pied Piper Apples

KEEP REFRIGERATED

KEEP REFRIGERATED

PERISHABLE-HANDLE WITH CARE

Delaware Development Office

Delaware Development Office

With all that industry in such a small state, it's amazing that there is room left for natural beauty. And yet, Delaware has ten state parks, four state forests, and a National Wildlife Refuge that covers 16,000 acres along the Delaware Bay. Rehoboth Beach, a peaceful town in southern Delaware, has a population of 1,730 in the winter and fifty times that in the summer. Tourists make a healthy contribution to Delaware's income.

Rehoboth Beach (left), Delaware's famous ocean resort, is contrasted with another tourist attraction—fishing on Silver Lake (above).

In addition to such places to visit as the Nemours Mansion and Gardens (left) and the Bombay Hook National Wildlife Refuge (below), Delaware offers the simple, natural beauty of the countryside (above).

Willard Stewart, Inc.

Small World, No Walls

"Something that everyone strives for is to feel as though you are belonging. And to deliberately do something which sets one apart and builds a barrier between friends and strangers to me is counterproductive. . . . Picture yourself in a chauffer-driven limousine. You lose contact with everybody. You drive down the street, they look at you as though there is something wrong with you."

Irénée Éleuthére du Pont, Jr., doesn't have to drive a 1963 Chevrolet station wagon. He lives in the great du Pont family mansion and could afford chauffer-driven limousines without any trouble. But that's not the way things are done in Delaware. The fewer walls there are between people here, the better they like it. And that goes for du Ponts as well as for Smiths.

Irénée Éleuthére du Pont, Jr., is shown against the background of Brandywine Creek State Park in autumn.

Pierre S. du Pont IV—Pete—explains that it goes for government, too. He ought to know. He's governor of the state of Delaware.

"In 1977, Delaware had perhaps the worst fiscal performance of all fifty states in America. We were at the bottom of the pile—the highest tax rate, the lowest credit rating. And we came to recognize, with the leaders of the legisla-

ture, that we were all in this together. And instead of one of us putting water into the boat, we decided to take our buckets and everybody bail water out."

So the political leaders of Delaware decided to forget about who was a Republican and who was a Democrat, who was going to get credit for solving the problems, and who was going to get blamed. Businesses were impressed.

"They were astonished that here in one room were all the decision makers, including the mayor and governor, who would directly impact the things that were going to happen to their business in Delaware."

That kind of cooperation turned Delaware around economically. Its financial situation is now one of the best in the country. And that kind of attitude—no walls—operates on a smaller scale, too. Take the day Governor du Pont moved into his new office.

"It's Saturday, been governor six days and the phone rings. Well, all the secretaries are there in their blue jeans carrying things around so I answer the phone. 'I'd like to speak to the governor, please.' 'Speaking.' 'Look, governor, I live up on Newark, and we had a terrible rainstorm last night and my basement is full of water and I want you to help.' . . . That's the kind of state it is, and where else in America would you find people who think when their basement's full of water that the thing to do is call the governor?"

Governor Pete du Pont (left) is shown against the governor's mansion and the Dover Days Celebration on The Green in New Castle.

City Homesteaders

"I was here because Sally was going to school here. When we saw this homesteading program, we put in for a house. But I was thinking there's some catch here. People don't give away houses. But they did. It's still going on. You just have to walk around and look at the For Sale signs."

All of this country's big cities have slums. And all of those cities have tried one thing after another to solve the problem. Wilmington, Delaware, came up with the kind of solution you would expect from the people of this small, creative state. The city started giving houses away. The city offered to give away—

The photograph below shows Terry O'Byrne working on a doorway.

Karl Longberg-Holm

Terry and a worker are shown working in the sunroom (left), and on the right, Sally and Terry are putting in French Doors.

or to sell at extremely low prices—abandoned houses to anyone who would fix them up and live in them. Terry and Sally O'Byrne bought a house early in the program.

"Every day I look in the paper or I talk to real estate people, and they're buying houses for five thousand, fifteen hundred, dollars. Which anyone with a little perseverance can put the money together to buy. And then all you have to do is use your own abilities to fix it up."

Mike and Paulette Bennefield came later, from Detroit. It's not just getting a house for fifteen hundred dollars that Paulette finds exciting.

"It's a good feeling to be part of something that seems to be beginning. And it's real exciting to be at the forefront of that and out there in the midst of it. There is going to be an awful lot of good things happening in this city. . . . This is going to be home for us. We are very comfortable here and we've taken root. We like it."

Wilmington likes it, too. What city wouldn't rather have families like the O'Byrnes and the Bennefields than empty, abandoned houses?

The Crafty State of Delaware

There is a huge, beautiful building outside Wilmington, Delaware. It is called Winterthur. Inside it are 125 rooms out of the past. And each room is filled with chairs, tables, china, silver—all made by early American craftspeople.

Winterthur was founded by Henry Francis du Pont. It is typical of the culture of Delaware, showing an appreciation for the past, for this country, and for the creations of people who work with their hands. Those things are valued in Delaware.

This small state has also produced a number of people who have been important in the educational and literary life of the country. The *Saturday Review,* one of the most important literary magazines in the United States, was founded by

A miniature stair hall in the Winterthur Museum.

Henry Seidel Canby, who was born in Delaware. He was also its first editor and a well-known author in his own right. Like other Delaware authors, Canby was an educator.

Samuel Miller, an early resident of Delaware, and Jay Saunders Redding, who wrote *On Being Negro in America,* were other important Delaware author-educators.

But perhaps Delaware's best-known and best-loved writer was Howard Pyle. His books for young people, including *The Wonder Clock* and *The Merry Adventures of Robin Hood,* are filled with his wonderful, humor-filled illustrations. The Delaware Art Museum is proud of its fine collection of Pyle's paintings and illustrations.

North of Wilmington is the village of Arden, which was founded in 1900 with a strong interest in arts and crafts. The village still regularly produces the plays of Shakespeare and operettas of Gilbert and Sullivan.

There are theater and music groups in towns all over the state. And many of them are made up of the people of those communities. As with so many other things, the people of Delaware tend to like to make their art themselves.

Shown below is a scene from a production of the theater in Arden.

Peter J. Wilson

*At the right is Howard Pyle, with
one of his paintings in the background.*

At Home
with the Chickens

"When I got drafted in the Army, my father, who I'd farmed with until that point, took me to the bus to go off to the Army. I said good-bye. I leaned in the door and said to him, 'Well, you'll never see me back on that mudhole again.' But I wasn't gone too long before I wanted to come back. I've been here ever since."

It was not just chickens and grain that brought Joe Hughes back to the farm. It was a feeling.

At the right is Joe Hughes' farm with some chickens in the foreground.

Office of Ag Communications
Delware Cooperative Extension Service

It has to do with being close to the land. It also has to do with making what you need and use. Like the baskets Joe Hughes makes.

"The greatest satisfaction in basketry is the fact that you can go into the woods once you know how to do it, find the proper tree, cut that tree down, tear it apart pretty much with your bare hands, and make something useful out of it."

That's a satisfaction that people who work with their hands often talk about. Whether the craft is basket-making, weaving, carpentry, or quilting, there is something about making things from scratch that is healing. It's a rare feeling in the modern world.

". . . when I sit here and make baskets, I feel it's very much a timeless thing. I could be here a hundred years ago doing this. It's a complete escape from the modern world and all its associated technology.

"I'm in touch with the past and with something that's now. There is a very strong feeling here of languishing in

On the left-hand page is a photograph of Joe Hughes sitting at a knifehorse, which lets him use a knife while leaving both hands free. Above, he is splitting white oak for use in a basket.

that completeness and not going to look for something else far away from here. It makes me feel very comfortable."

41

A Big Future
for a Small State

"**I** am convinced that Delaware has the potential
to become a Model State. The state that started a nation can
also lead a nation."

Those optimistic words of former governor Russell Peterson speak well for the people of Delaware. Faced with one of
the worst financial situations in the country in 1977, Delaware has completely turned itself around. Today, the unemployment rate is well below the national average, incomes
are above, and taxes are low.

Industrially, Delaware is growing by leaps and bounds.
But that growth presents special problems for a state this
size. Is there room for more than 250 companies in a state
that is smaller than some Indian reservations? So far, the

Wilmington in the fall.

Delaware's industrial growth all takes place within the context of strict pollution laws.

answer seems to be yes. But it is going to take wisdom on the part of the leaders, and the people, of Delaware to make things work.

Some of that wisdom is already at work. Delaware was one of the first states to pass strict pollution laws. It passed the Coastal Zone Act to prevent any heavy industrial development along the state's coast. Today, Delaware has one of the most natural coastal areas of any of the mid-dle Atlantic states. The challenge is to keep it that way.

Well-paid employment is important to the quality of life anywhere. Delaware has that. But there are other factors. Clean air. Unspoiled coasts and marshes. Respect for the past and its creations. Delaware has those, too. If it can carefully juggle all these elements, the future looks bright for this gem of a state.

Important Historical Events in Delaware

1609 Henry Hudson goes through the Delaware Bay to explore the Delaware River.

1610 Samuel Argall names the bay after Virginia Governor Lord De La Warr.

1631 The first European settlement in Delaware is made by the Dutch at Zwaanendael, now Lewes.

1632 The settlement is destroyed by the Leni-Lenape, or Delaware, Indians.

1638 Swedish colonists led by Peter Minuit build Fort Christina, now Wilmington. It is the first permanent settlement in Delaware.

1643-
1653 Dutch members of the New Sweden Company withdraw from the colony.

1655 The Dutch governor of New Amsterdam sends forces to conquer New Sweden and incorporates it into the New Amsterdam colony.

1664 In order to eliminate Dutch competition in trading with the American colonies, the British attack Dutch colonies. Delaware becomes part of the province of New York.

1682 The Duke of York gives the Delaware counties to William Penn, founder of Pennsylvania.

1704 Penn permits the people of Delaware to form their own legislature. They share Pennsylvania's governor but make their own laws.

1739 The Borough of Wilmington is given a royal charter.

1776 Delaware delegates sign the Declaration of Independence. Delaware writes its own constitution.

1777 The British army invades Delaware on its way from the Chesapeake Bay to Philadelphia. After the British seize Wilmington, the capital is moved from New Castle to Dover.

1787 Delaware is the first state to ratify the United States Constitution.

1792 The second state constitution is ratified.

1802 The Du Pont industrial empire is founded when E.I. du Pont opens a gun powder mill on the Brandywine.

1812 James A. Bayard, a Delaware congressman, serves on the peace commission in opposition to the War of 1812.

1829 The free school act is passed. Two Canals, the Chesapeake and the Delaware, are opened.

1831 The third state constitution is passed.

1861 Although a slave state, Delaware refuses to secede from the Union.

1897 The fourth, and present, state constitution is adopted.

1924 A highway that runs the entire length of the state is built.

1951 The Delaware Memorial Bridge links Delaware with New Jersey.

1966 The large population of New Castle County forces a reorganization of the county government.

1968 The legislature is reapportioned.

1971 The Delaware Coastal Zone Act forbids construction of industrial plants in the coastal area of Delaware.

Delaware Almanac

Nickname. The First State.

Capital. Dover.

State Bird. Blue hen chicken.

State Flower. Peach Blossom.

State Tree. American holly.

State Motto. Liberty and independence.

State Song. Our Delaware.

State Abbreviations. Del. (traditional); DE (postal).

Statehood. December 7, 1787, the first state.

Government. Congress: U.S. senators, 2; U.S. representatives, 1. **State Legislature:** senators, 21; representatives, 41. **Counties:** 3.

Area. 2,057 sq. mi. (5,328 sq. km.), 49th in size among the states.

Greatest Distances. north/south, 96 mi. (155 km.); east/west, 35 mi. (56 km.). **Coastline:** 28 mi. (45 km.).

Elevation. Highest: 442 ft. (135 m). **Lowest:** sea level, along the coastline.

Population. 1980 Census: 595, 225 (7.9% increase over 1970), 47th among the states. **Density:** 289 persons per sq. mi. (112 persons per sq. km.). **Distribution:** 71% urban, 29% rural. **1970 Census:** 548,104.

Economy. Agriculture: soybeans, corn, potatoes, broilers. **Fishing Industry:** clams, crabs. **Manufacturing:** chemicals, food products, paper products, automobiles, apparel, luggage. **Mining:** magnesium, sand and gravel.

Places to Visit

Amstel House in New Castle.

Hagley Museum Historic Site, near Wilmington.

Henry Francis du Pont Winterthur Museum, near Wilmington.

Iron Hill, near Newark.

Old Swedes Church in Wilmington.

Rehoboth Beach in Rehoboth.

State House in Dover.

Zwaanendael Museum in Lewes.

Annual Events

Swedish Colonial Day in Wilmington (March).

Boardwalk Fashion Promenade at Rehoboth Beach (Easter Sunday).

A Day in Old New Castle (May).

State Fair in Harrington (July).

Autumn and Christmas tours at Hagley Museum, near Wilmington (October and December).

Delaware 500 stock car race in Dover (September).

Delaware Day, statewide (December 7).

Delaware Counties

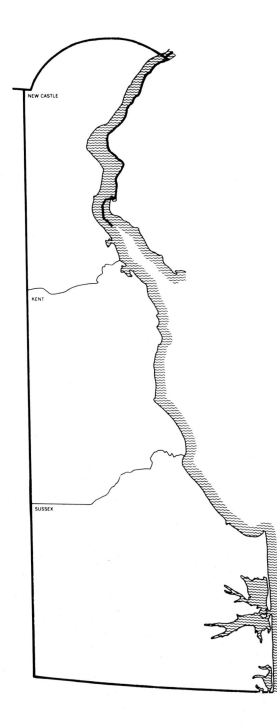

NEW CASTLE

KENT

SUSSEX

INDEX